Grandma's Guide to a Happy Marriage

Mary McBride
with Veronica McBride

Illustrated by Christine Tripp

Published by BROTHERS GRIMM PUBLISHING

Library of Congress Cataloguing-in-Publication Data

Satire

Library of Congress No. 91-070370

ISBN No.: 0-9627601-1-0

Editor: Helen Duffy

About the Authors: Mary McBride has been a gag writer for Phyllis Diller and Joan Rivers and is one of the busiest and funniest speakers in America. She and her daughter, Veronica McBride, have also written ***Grandma Knows Best, But No One Ever Listens!, Don't Call Mommy at Work Today Unless the Sitter Runs Away, The Empty Nest Symphony, and Grandma's Guide to Child Care.***

About the Illustrator: Christine Tripp has illustrated the previous McBride books and lives with her husband and four children in Ottawa, Canada.

Table of Contents

Chapter 1
There Isn't an ELIGIBLE MEN Listing in the Phone Book

ou could meet Mr. Right by attending night school —
man might notice you if beside him you're sitting,
But when you sign up you'd better make sure
Your courses aren't sewing or knitting.

fore you can use a Marriage Guide you must have
usband.

ding a man you want to marry and who wants to rry you can be an arduous undertaking. There- e, a little help toward this objective could be in ler.

ars ago there was not a Husband/Wife Wanted tion in Classified, but now that is the part of the er many young people look at first.

ver consider a boring ad, because you can be e whoever placed it will be even more boring in son. Ignore the ad that reads, "I am interested in eting someone who doesn't smoke or drink, likes lance and also enjoys quiet times."

attention to something like, "Tired of coming oss with so much income tax? Get a charming, dsome deduction," or, "Do you really enjoy ng alone in front of a warm, crackling fire?"

The following are a few more suggestions of how to meet a man who could become your husband:

Join a service club that has just started to permit women to belong.

Live in a warm climate. Being outside gives more opportunities to meet people.

Start a USO for your local Army Reserve.

At public meetings vote "Nay!" instead of "Aye!". You will be noticed.

Look for a dentist who doesn't wear a wedding ring. Say that you're afraid a ring will scratch your mouth.

There are many ways to meet a man.

Join a choral group and try out for an alto part. The altos stand next to the baritones.

Hang around airports. A man waiting for someone whose flight has been delayed might be interested in having a cup of coffee with you.

Have a cure for hiccoughs or laryngitis. If you come across a man who has either of these problems, you can start a conversation with him.

Memorize men's names in divorce columns.

Become a census taker, and you can find out who is single.

Become a legal secretary. You are apt to meet a man who is getting a divorce.

Get on a game show. Contestants always hug each other.

If a man drives away and you get his parking space, blow him a kiss.

Buy bait. There will no doubt be other men buying bait.

Move the mall bench so you can sit in front of the Men's Clothing Store.

Buy an expensive diary. This will make you try harder to meet someone so you'll have something worthwhile to write in it.

There are certain things you should not do in the search of a mate:

Don't have a fuzz buster. You could meet an attractive State Trooper.

Don't have a suitcase you pull on wheels. A man might say, "Could I carry that bag for you?"

Don't have a bumper sticker that reads MY FATHER IS RICH.

Men don't like women who are too obvious in their pursuit of a husband.

Don't jump overboard if you go on a cruise and you find there is not one eligible man.

If he promises to call, and when he finally does it's for bail money, forget him!

Chapter 2

The Wedding — A Legal Game of Chance

Your groom is a bit immature
If he's suggested — in fact, insisted
When registering for gifts that are wanted
Your name in a toy store be listed.

The relationship between the man and woman is more important than the details of the wedding, although many brides-to-be believe the opposite is true.

Planning the wedding should be a romantic interlude filled with happy anticipation. Too often it is a miserable time with tempers flaring.

Reading a whole book of etiquette can be overwhelming and add to the tension. However, a wedding **is** an important event, and many details must be considered.

The following are a few suggestions that may not be in a book but could make for a better celebration:

After he proposes, you accept and he kisses you, think, "Cut!" End the kiss, and rush to the phone to try to book a hall for the reception.

Be sure not to pick a date that is the same day as an important sporting event. He may call it off unless you can find a priest, minister or rabbi who will permit a TV on the altar.

It doesn't look good for the marriage if the groom strays at the reception.

Some couples do have two ceremonies but never so the bride can wear her hair up during one and down during the other. It has to be for the purpose of religion.

Try to plan something distinctive, so it isn't the same as all other weddings. For instance, instead of a camcorder, have an artist sketch the bride and groom at the altar.

Insist the best man rent a tuxedo instead of wearing one of his own suits so there is no chance of losing the ring because of a hole in his pocket.

Tell your father to take slow, measured steps as he escorts you down the aisle. Otherwise, the groom will wonder why he is in such a hurry.

At the rehearsal, make sure everyone understands his or her part. Congestion on the altar detracts from the beauty of the wedding.

It is better not to have the honeymoon be a cruise. The wonderful food may make it impossible for him to carry you over the threshold.

To some men the word "commitment" is like fingernails on a blackboard. They act as if they are giving up a throne. The groom may go so far as to back out after the wedding date has been set.

A girl often is so in love with love that she does not notice that her intended has a serious case of cold feet. Even if he doesn't appear again after the proposal, she is sure he'll show up for the wedding.

It is better to be prepared that the nuptials will not take place. The following are a few signals that your beloved may not go through with it:

He frequently says, "What's a piece of paper?"

He talks about a previous engagement as a near-death experience.

He starts to sweat and shake every time he hears honks from wedding cars.

He doesn't return your call, and you called from a hospital.

He asks you to wear gloves, because looking at your engagement ring makes him nervous.

Your picture on his desk has been replaced by a picture of his bowling team.

He stops playing with your niece and nephew.

You go to a restaurant, and he suggests the counter instead of a booth or table.

Every time he sits down, he pats his knee for his dog to jump up on his lap.

On the altar, he blinks his eyes, shakes his head and asks, "Where am I?!"

Even though he gets his nerves under control, and the wedding takes place, the marriage may not turn out as great as you anticipated. The following are a few tip-offs that your picture will not be in the paper for being married 50 years:

You start throwing plates at each other in the department store when you are picking out your china pattern.

He moves his place card at the wedding table so he is sitting between two bridesmaids.

He asks the clergyman to read the pre-nuptial agreement to the guests.

You say, "I do," and he whispers, "Your voice has too high a pitch."

He sets up dinner dates with former girl friends to tell them he is married.

Before you insist upon a hyphenated name, measure your mailbox to see if it will fit.

Chapter 3

Mothers-in-Law Do Not Make Good House Pets

When the phone rings and I hear
My mother-in-law with her chiding
I would prefer it to be
A person selling siding.

All in-laws are different, but they usually have one thing in common — thinking their children could have married better.

Therefore, it isn't strange that the word "mother-in-law" doesn't give rise to sentimental feelings. You might note there has never been a song written about a mother-in-law.

Mothers-in-law are not known for building daughters'-in-law self-esteem.

The in-law situation could easily be the worst part of your marriage. In fact, it might be wise to search for a woman you would like to have for a mother-in-law who has a son you could marry.

Your mother-in-law is apt to feel that you are playing hooky from your responsibilities as a wife and mother.

There are many ways your mother-in-law may show she considers you an under-achiever. The following are a few examples:

The only plant she ever gives you is a cactus.

You serve Jell-o, and she raves about how much your cooking has improved.

She asks your children to call her if they are ever hungry.

She has your son call her every time he gets heartburn.

She closes her eyes while she is eating your meal.

She wipes her feet as she leaves your house.

You should realize this treatment is common, and you must try not to get upset.

Also, there are things you can do to have a better mother-in-law, daughter-in-law relationship:

Survey friends. Find out what they do to get along with their mothers-in-law.

A mother-in-law can let it be known you are an under-achiever.

Make her a role model. Watch her to see how you can some day instill fear in the heart of your daughter-in-law.

Instead of thinking of her as a meddling busybody, try to look on her as a wise person, willing and able to solve every problem.

If she is on tranquilizers, have a duplicate bottle of her prescription at your house.

Ask her to accompany you to PTA meetings, so she will feel she has a say-so in raising your children.

Be phony. Say things like, "My day is not complete until we've talked."

Have her show you how to do things. Even if you're a nurse, have her show you how to read a thermometer.

Take her attention away from your cooking. Have her grandchildren perform while she's eating.

If you are the only in-law in town, it might occur to you to have her bussed to other in-laws. This cannot be done.

There are other no-no's — no matter how difficult your mother-in-law is:

Don't take her glasses to clean and leave a film so she can't see flaws.

Don't suggest she take estrogen, tranquilizers or switch to de-caffeinated coffee.

Don't give her a budget sheet to show her how much of the family income you contribute.

Don't write to Ann Landers about her, and sign your real name.

Don't challenge her to a formal debate.

"Just say 'No'" doesn't apply to a suggestion by your mother-in-law.

Chapter 4

The Thermometer-Toting Wife

He turns into a child and a yeller
The minute he becomes infirm,
But instead of hating the man
Try hard to hate just the germ.

It's nice to have a man around the house — but not when he's sick.

Waiting on your husband during an illness is intense stuff.

If you're a registered nurse, he won't feel you're giving him adequate care.

You can squeeze oranges for orange juice, polish the apple you give him, put a flower on his tray — but nothing will be enough.

Royalty doesn't expect as much service as a sick husband.

It's nice when the doctor gives it to you straight — "He's sick, and he's going to be ornery until he gets well."

As the illness goes on, he becomes a dictator — "Bring me a glass of water ... Turn the channel ... Get me another pillow ..."

It might help to know that your husband is not unusual in how he handles being sick.

The following are a few statements wives have made about their sick husbands:

> "The doctor gave him a clean bill of health, and he reported the doctor to the AMA."

Husbands seldom show their most mature selves during an illness.

"I told him his temperature was normal, and he acted like I was an umpire who made a bad call."

"He's 55, and he reported me for abuse to the elderly because I was 10 minutes getting back with his drink of water."

"He called a sliver he got on a picnic bench shrapnel."

"He says he shouldn't be declared well as long as there a shadow of a doubt he is sick."

"He yelled, 'Hey, Next of Kin, will you please fluff my pillow.'"

"He thinks he has to get a second opinion on his Ask-A-Nurse call."

"I'm sure he thinks my holding his head is more romantic than my holding his hand."

"He thought his illness was so fascinating, he expected a call back from his doctor."

"I feel like getting appendicitis for revenge."

The following are a few suggestions to help you get through your husband's illness with less discomfort:

Make him take an oath that he will tell you when he feels better.

Tell him if he rings the bell too often, he'll get Bell Ringer's Wrist.

Try to convince him the cold he has is not rare.

If your husband was in an accident, and an ambulance chaser comes to the door, tell him he can have the case if he helps wait on your husband.

Pretend you're a flight attendant.

Try to arouse his competitive spirit. Say, "You're taking your strep throat so much better than Art Lukas took his!"

Get the mailman to say, "You poor guy!"

If he says, "I think I'm coming down with something, so I'm going to stay home today," tell him there is no such thing as taking early sick leave.

Buy some great lunch box treats, so he'll be anxious to go back to work.

Wear a mileage meter so you can tell how many calories you've burned.

You really should ask, "Why him?" instead of asking, "Why me?" These mirthless days will bring forth many impulses unworthy of you. However, there are a few other things you shouldn't do, no matter how strong the urge:

Don't make threatening phone calls to the person who gave him the cold.

Don't put a teddy bear night light in his room to point out he's being a baby.

Don't get a T-shirt that reads, "I SURVIVED MY HUSBAND'S 10-DAY VIRUS."

Don't have HIS painted on the medicine chest.

Don't ask him more than five times a day, "When do you think you'll be going back to work?"

Happiness is seeing a toothpick coming out of his mouth instead of a thermometer.

Chapter 5

Don't Hide Your Purchases Until They're Out of Style

If you want a rain-and-shine coat
Don't ask and say, "What do you think?"
You'll get much quicker approval
If you start by requesting a mink.

Money is on the top of the list of things about which husbands and wives fight.

In most cases a wife is more extravagant than her husband, who is on the conservative side and wants her to be.

It helps to think that your husband is worried about your being someday left alone without adequate funds.

Countless husbands are unhappy about the way money is spent. The following are some comments made by women with frugal husbands:

"He won't let me clean, because he thinks dust acts as insulation."

"They are starting to put the chairs on top of the tables by the time he gets through re-figuring the bill."

"If we were Adam and Eve, he'd try to get me to go to a used clothing store."

"He untied that garbage bag 20 times to get in one more item."

"He would rather have had our son join a street gang than that fraternity, because there are no dues."

"He asked the hostess if there was a difference in price between the smoking and non-smoking sections."

"I have never heard anyone say to my husband, 'You forgot your change, Sir.'"

"He's trying to talk me into becoming an agoraphobic."

"He said, 'We get THE SHOPPER — why do we need another paper?'"

Very few husbands are casual about spending money.

"When he reaches for his wallet, it's always only to check and see that it's there."

"His whole family is cheap. His brother informed us of their mother's death by a collect call."

When you have a cheap husband, you will have to adjust to him. You cannot change him. If he won the lottery 10 times, he would still be stingy.

There are signals that you have a cheap husband. The following are a few tip-offs:

He gets hysterical when a magician cuts a bill in half.

He wears an I GAVE AT THE OFFICE T-shirt.

He counts tax write-offs to get to sleep at night.

He asks for a discount on the bill from the obstetrician, because he coached you during the delivery.

He tries to tell you credit cards cause cancer.

When you want a bigger house, he suggests you just wallpaper with horizontal stripes to make the rooms look bigger.

No matter how good an example of spending money you give him, he will still be cheap.

It won't work to tell him that the money he gives you is tax deductible, but there are other things you can do so there will be less fighting over the spending of money.

Try to keep him healthy, so he won't be home when your bills arrive.

Have the waiter give him the amount of the check after the drinks, after the appetizers, after the entree and after the dessert, so he isn't so shocked at the end.

Get a taller spindle, so it looks like you have fewer bills.

Have a secret compartment in your clothes closet where you can hide clothes you don't want your husband to know about.

Just as comedians are better off if they are ready with ad libs, wives are wise to be prepared with excuses for their shopping excursions.

Tell him, "I took a wrong turn and ended up at Bloomingdale's."

Say, "No self-respecting woman would have stayed away from that sale."

Try to make him feel sorry for retailers.

Say, "At that price it was a good buy if I never wore it once."

Tell him that if you're ever missing, you know he would want to be able to describe you as wearing something fashionable.

Say, "When you left this morning, you told me to have a nice day."

Shop at sales, and tell him the more you shop the more you save.

Explain that you want to teach your daughter how to shop, and the best way to do that is to let her watch you shop.

Eat more or eat less, so your clothes won't fit.

To help your husband overcome his cheapness, try applauding when he parts with money. You can't clap in church when he drops something in the collection box so just mouth, "Good!"

Chapter 6

Getting Blue Over Blueprints

Don't give your husband the hammer
When you decide you are going to build —
You'll end up saying, "You're clumsy!"
Better to hire someone who's skilled.

When you look at a house, you never think of all the arguments that went into its being built.

Fights over building keep marriage counselors in business.

Husbands go through stages when you suggest building a house — anger, denial, and finally, acceptance.

Some sample excuses husbands use to avoid the trials of putting up a new home are, "We'll be evicting kids from a baseball diamond, and they'll get into trouble," or "It'll be years before our mail will catch up to us."

If interest rates change more than 20 times he is dragging his feet too long, and you should work harder on coming up with convincing arguments for a new house. The following are a few suggestions:

> "We'll have to go on a strict diet, because we won't fit into this house."

> "TV reception for sporting events would be better in another house."

Suggest that the entertainment center be built last.

"This whole house is on the blink!"

Tell your husband what the house would cost in pesos, and then tell him the amount in dollars. The contract will make it seem cheap.

Practice makes perfect, but he can't build 25 houses, so it is better to hire professionals to do the jobs about which your husband knows nothing.

However, you would save a little money if he did some of the work. One way to get him to pitch in would be to have him become interested in weightlifting, and paint 150 lbs. on 2' x 4's.

The following are some tips that could help you have a happier house-building experience.

Look at homes the builder built previously. If this is his first house, ask if you can see what he did with his Lincoln Logs and erector set.

Get a post office box where the bills can be sent, so your husband won't see them.

More important than worrying about how the house faces the sun is making sure it doesn't face a sunbather.

Have the guarantees staggered, so you won't have to replace the roof, the furnace and the water heater all at the same time.

Take out an FHA loan. The government will set down the building rules, so you and your husband won't have to argue over decisions.

Select bright colors. Then, if your husband doesn't like the shade of paint you chose, tell him it will fade.

If you have a mirrored ceiling in your bedroom, have it reversible so it can be a non-mirrored one after you reach 50.

Tell your husband to be careful not to fall down a stairwell where steps have not yet been built. He won't be wearing a parachute.

Have the bookshelves, TV area and bar built last. Otherwise, your husband may just sit down and enjoy himself.

Still ahead will be the landscaping. Try to plan the building so it will be finished in the winter, and you will have a bit of time before starting on yard arguments.

Husbands tend to be conservative in planning. The following are a few tips on how to get your dream house.

If you want a swimming pool, find a doctor who will say you need to swim so you can deduct it from your income tax.

If your husband says something is too expensive, tell him you had a credit check run on him and he can afford it.

Suggest an extra bedroom instead of a guest room. Guest room will make him think of company and expense.

If you have children, get them to say, "Please, Daddy!"

Have friends over to back up your ideas.

Tell him he may become famous, and hordes of people will drive by the house.

If you don't get the things you have your heart set on, tell yourself it won't be as hard should you have to move.

Chapter 7

Does He Keep One Hand on the Wheel and One Over your Mouth?

You'd think that thoughts of vacation
Would be something nice to savor,
But often forgetting it fast
Is doing yourself a favor.

It's hard to believe that a car, which at one time was the setting for romance, could ever become the site of arguments.

However, when you go on a driving trip with your husband, continuously getting along comes close to being impossible.

You will be better natured if you do what you enjoy, but what you enjoy could be something your husband doesn't. Therefore you must be tricky about getting your way.

You can't call a sale a tourist attraction but you can say, "All the best restaurants are in malls."

The following are some additional tips to make your trip more enjoyable:

It's good to start out early but not so early that you'll feel your husband has not yet reached the age of reason. Notice the time of day his good-naturedness kicks in and have your wake-up call for then.

Have an extra fan belt in your suitcase.

Put tape over the speedometer and gas gauge so you don't keep saying, "Slow down!" and "Don't you think we should stop for gas?"

If he thinks touring ruins will be boring, tell him there'll be great graffiti.

It is better to squint than drive back 20 miles to retrieve your sunglasses.

Your fighting will be more noticeable in a small town than in a big city.

Tell him you'll run his bath water for him at the motel if he'll stop and ask for directions.

It is very difficult to get a man to ask for directions.

Realize he is tired of listening to you talk if he stops along the way to have a telephone installed and tells you to call people.

It is common for husbands and wives to spell each other on long trips, so it is wise for you to be prepared for your husband's criticism of your driving. For instance, a husband never takes for granted that his wife will stop at a stop sign.

The following are a few ideas of how you can survive your husband sitting beside you when you are at the wheel:

Order warm milk for him when you stop, so he'll fall asleep when you're driving.

Have something hanging from the mirror. It could hypnotize him.

Pretend he's a stern drivers' education teacher.

Get a CB handle, and make your husband use that instead of your name. It won't seem like he's yelling at you.

Turn the car's air conditioner to maximum. You want him to be as cool as possible.

Drive carefully, so you don't damage the car. Only one husband in a million will say, "This old crate?! Who cares?!!"

The following are a few no-no's for an automobile sojourn with your husband:

Don't throw away pop cans. Keep them for squeezing to vent your feelings.

Don't flirt with road-building crews.

Don't point out beautiful views when your husband is lost.

Don't suggest singing when your husband is lost.

Don't roll down the window and yell, "Help! We're lost!" when your husband is lost.

Don't comparative price shop for gas when the gauge is on E.

Don't wear anything that is black and white checked. He may drive too fast.

Don't have a liberal talk show host on the radio if he is conservative or vice versa. He may take his feelings out on the traffic.

Don't suggest a short cut to your husband unless you've gone that way at least 50 times.

Don't beg for overnight lodging at a Tourist Information building.

Don't have the newspaper stopped while you're gone. You may not be speaking when you get home, and it would be nice to have something to read.

There isn't a boss anywhere that will count two weeks' vacation as only one because you had a rotten time.

Chapter 8

Dot the I's with Hearts on the Chore List

If you clean and scrub together
You might make your husband jealous
If when you look at hands
Your hand has the bigger callous.

Once upon a time when men were at home, they were only called upon to do "men" things like opening jars and oiling squeaking hinges.

But finally, women woke up to the fact that men were enjoying meals, clean clothes and a neat house, so they should be equally responsible for these pleasures.

Gone is the image of Dagwood sleeping on the couch with his back to Blondie vacuuming. No longer is it enough for the husband to open the door for his wife when she gets home with the groceries.

However, since the theory is comparatively new, women must work to keep it in effect. Many men preferred the old way.

The following are a few samples of excuses men come up with for why they shouldn't share the work load:

I can't do the laundry, because I'm color blind and unable to sort.

I can't cook, because my attention span is so short I'd burn things.

Make scrubbing the floor into an athletic event.

I won't garden, because I prefer to send you flowers from the florist.

I can't change the baby, because I'm allergic to talcum powder.

I can't wash dishes, because my hands are so big my fingers get caught in cup handles.

I can't grocery shop, because I have a heavy hand on the cart and hit other shoppers' heels.

Men are apt to think of the hours they spend doing housework as "serving time."

Your husband might say, "The way you feel about housework is a sickness," but don't waiver.

The following are a few tips on how you can receive help from your husband and have a well-run household:

Make cleaning the house a business relationship. Have Articles of Partnership drawn up.

Start immediately after the wedding. Each wash off half the letters of JUST MARRIED.

Count the pieces of furniture that must be dusted and assign half to your husband. Then you can say "your dust" if it's on his furniture.

Have a different set of dishes for each of you and a different set of silverware. You can each be responsible for washing your own.

Buy matching cleaning outfits. Looking like professional cleaners could result in better work.

Make a rule that whoever has thrown the most items into the wastebasket has to empty it.

Put gold stars after chores completed well.

Put his chore list on the refrigerator door and duplicates on the medicine chest mirror, the bureau mirror, the TV screen, and leave it among the answering machine messages so he can't say, "I forgot."

If you are working together and he is sloppy about the way he does things, wear blinders.

Remember that in school **you** belonged to the Future Homemakers of America. He didn't.

Your husband may promise to vacuum for half an hour — the vacuum doesn't sound right, he spends 25 minutes investigating, and he wants to deduct that from his vacuuming time.

Therefore, you must appeal to his masculine instincts to get him to do his share.

Tell him dirt is the "bad guy" who brings disease to his wife and children. He'll feel heroic getting rid of it.

Distribute his trophies all over the house instead of keeping them on one shelf. He will make sure the areas around them are spiffed up.

Have a stopwatch going while he scrubs the floor or bathtub, and he can work to beat his own time.

Have a duck painted on the vacuum bag.

Permit profanity.

Pretend grocery shopping is a scavenger hunt.

Make birdwatching a competition. He'll make sure the windows are clean, so he doesn't miss a species.

Have him think of himself as an explorer going places where no one has gone before, like behind the refrigerator.

To encourage him to cook, buy brown eggs instead of white. They look more manly.

However, don't try to talk him into a scrubbing weekend instead of a skiing weekend.

He's come a long way if you find coupons when you empty his pockets.

Chapter 9

He Has to be Reminded that Children are Wonderful

Kids cause you so much worry
Time for self is something you will lack
But one good thing to come of it
You won't become a hypochondriac.

It is not smart to think that you will be happier after you have children.

Children are wonderful, but they do things that are upsetting to grown-ups. Therefore, it could happen that your marriage is a degree less happy than before you were blessed with offspring.

The changes are not all for the better. Your husband had you all to himself. Now he needs a bullhorn when he says, "Honey, I'm home!"

Women are born with more adjustable genes than men. Many fathers take kid problems very hard. It is a bright woman who makes these happenings seem less serious to her husband.

Every time he registers a complaint about the children, dismiss it with a positive statement. The following are a few examples:

HE: He's 25 and still doesn't know what he wants to do.

SHE: Keeping options open is great.

HE: We would have a hyperactive child.

SHE: Candid pictures are so much more interesting with a hyperactive child.

HE: They're always on the phone.

SHE: We're never bothered with wrong numbers or telephone sales people.

HE: He won't get a paper route.

SHE: I'm sure he would if newspapers printed only good things about people.

HE: They never let us get a whole night's sleep.

Be a human metal detector when it comes to finding silver linings.

SHE: If there's anything wrong in the house, waiting until morning to discover it could be disastrous.

HE: I hate his growing his hair down to his shoulders.

SHE: At least it's something he's not being sneaky about.

HE: She wrecked my car **again**!

SHE: Some people pay insurance premiums for years and never get a cent back.

HE: They keep having to go to the bathroom when we travel.

SHE: The car can get too hot, so tires blow and engines burn out if you never stop.

HE: We're going broke paying baby-sitters.

SHE: Having someone at the house while we're gone is cheap insurance.

HE: They never close the door.

SHE: That's why our house doesn't smell stale.

HE: Instead of reading the newspaper at night, I always have to help them with their homework.

SHE: Think how good you'll be at math and spelling when you go over it again and again.

HE: He always borrows my clothes.

SHE: It's nice you can see how those items look on someone else.

HE: Not one kid is amounting to anything.

SHE: We won't lose friends with a bragging Christmas letter.

HE: I can't believe how many drinks of water I have to bring her after she gets in bed.

SHE: All that flouride will save us money on the dentist's bills.

HE: Every time we take him anyplace he has a tantrum.

SHE: Do you realize how much he helps childless couples when he acts like that?

HE: Our son just called from the Police Department.

SHE: To think he only gets one call, and he calls us.

If your children aren't giving you any problems, don't brag about it. Save your applause until the end.

Chapter 10

Don't Let Him Get Looking-for-a Job Burn-Out

Tell him he'll get a job eventually
Of this fact you're really sure
Because there isn't such a thing
As earning unemployment tenure.

Sometimes businesses do not do well and have cutbacks, sometimes they are sold and the buyer brings in his own people and sometimes businesses go out of existence. Your husband could become unemployed. He has no control over the business for which he works.

He will be a helpless victim. The whole world will look miserable to him.

You must work to build his self-esteem.

Tell him you didn't fall in love with him because of his job. (This will be easier to do if it was a high school romance.)

Throw out his Alumni News.

Rave about how well he takes messages while you are at work. Say, "That person probably would have hung up on our answering machine and never called back."

Say, "We owe almost nothing," and don't add, "If you compare it to the National Debt."

It is a good wife who builds her husband's self-esteem when he is unemployed.

Tell him all the divorces you know of that occurred because husbands were married to their jobs.

Say, "It's not for myself that I want you to get another job. It's so you can have all things I want for you."

If you get a promotion, don't let him know. Tell him the extra money in your check is a mistake and they will eventually catch it.

Promise him that the night he gets a job you'll have dinner by candlelight. Be sure you don't add, "And if you don't get a job, we'll have candlelight every night but no dinner."

Naturally, you will be relieved when he is again a contributor to the household treasury. There are some practical things you can do when the "for poorer" part of your marriage goes into effect.

Tear out the yellow pages of the phone book, so he doesn't call to have anything done professionally.

Tell him to shine his shoes so he can see his face in them. In that way he'll notice if he needs a haircut and you won't have to mention that, too.

If it's your birthday say, "Just a card is fine. I always break a nail unwrapping a gift."

He needs friends. Entertain by having a potluck dinner. For pride's sake, make them take their leftovers home with them.

There are other things you can do during this period of unemployment stress:

Go out and buy him a gold watch so he won't feel bad thinking he'll never get one.

Have his diploma cleaned and glazed.

Buy him shoes with industrial strength soles for pounding the pavement.

Hire a professional to produce his resumé. You can't count on getting a soft-hearted interviewer who'll say, "This poor guy has such a pathetic resumé, we've just got to give him a job."

If he goes to the library to look at help-wanted ads in newspapers, make him promise to read the comics right before he comes home.

Being a helpmate gives you the right to tell him there are things he should not do in his job search.

Tell him not to give as reasons for wanting the job:

"I have a heavy bet with a friend that I'll land this job."

"My wife is at work all day, and I'm lonesome."

If it's a woman interviewer, he shouldn't kiss her hand.

He must not ask for his resumé back.

He shouldn't act too eager such as bringing along x-rays with his physical report.

It is important that he doesn't have liquor on his breath during the interview, but he doesn't have to abstain the entire previous week.

It is all right to ask if they have medical insurance, but he should do it this way: "I'm never sick and this is a moot point, but do you have a health plan?"

Accentuate the positive. On April 15, go out and celebrate because you had to pay less income tax.

Chapter 11

It Doesn't Help to be the First to Know

When you tell him you know
With whom he's hobnobbing
Don't expect him to fall
At your knees loudly sobbing.

You must face the fact that there are husbands that can't be trusted. Some men can make square dancing into dirty dancing.

If your husband is one of the less trustworthy, there is a good chance that somewhere along the road of living happily ever after another woman will lure him away from you.

The following are a few tip-offs that your husband is having an affair:

He tells you that they have just inaugurated a policy at work that wives can't drop in.

He has lipstick on his collar, and he explains it is his mother's because her eyesight is getting bad.

He makes a List of Things to do and he has "kiss my wife" on it.

He asks you to wear a name tag.

He takes his wedding ring box with him when he leaves the house.

When confronted about having an affair, some husbands admit it. Others try to make you think you need estrogen.

If you have had it with the man, you may not wish to pursue a campaign to get him back.

Make a list of reasons why you want to have him return. Hopefully there will be at least one other than his employer's health insurance.

If there are enough to make you think it is worth the scheming and planning it would take to step back into Number 1 place in his heart you might find help in the following suggestions:

The cheating husband may have trouble remembering names.

Tell him the atmosphere in the house will be so chilly, the heat bills will go sky high.

Get 5,000 signatures on a petition that he leave her and come back to you.

Get famous, so a gossip magazine will print the story of the affair.

Buy a tombstone, and have both your names engraved on it.

While you feel he has committed a crime that warrants capital punishment, it might be a good idea to be wonderful enough that he wants to be by your side instead of hers.

Make him feel so important that he will think she isn't good enough for him.

Take money from the sugar bowl to have the loose step fixed instead of nagging him to do it.

Try every diet anyone suggests.

Get him a subscription to men's magazines such as FIELD AND STREAM or POPULAR MECHANICS, get him SPORTS ILLUSTRATED if you can get them to hold the swimsuit edition.

The following are some suggestions adhering to the adage, "All's fair in love and war":

Make it more difficult for them to have a secret rendezvous by moving to a small town and getting him a vanity license plate.

If he gave her a mink coat, have the animal rights people picket her house.

Buy identical clothes, and get a similar hairdo to the other woman so he gets sick of her.

Have her income tax audited.

Hire a private detective to catch them together. The FBI won't investigate for you.

Don't throw your wedding ring in his face. Sell it, or give it to GOODWILL.

Chapter 12

Don't Tell Him About Your Class Reunion Ahead of Time

If you go to your reunion alone
And he watches you fixing your face
He'll feel a lot better about it
If he looks in your purse and sees mace.

It is a black day for your husband when you tell him you expect him to attend your class reunion with you.

Attending a class reunion with your spouse when you are not a member of the class should be listed among the causes of greatest stress along with death, divorce and losing a job.

Put yourself in his place. If a lot of women you didn't know came up to your husband to hug and kiss him, **you'd** be miserable.

He rather feels like he's being invited to an orgy where he will be an onlooker and you a participant.

Many things can add to his apprehension. For instance, he will expect a really wild crowd if it is your year that is painted on the city's water tower.

The class reunion rules your life for a long period of time. You say things like, "We have to be careful — I don't want to go to the reunion pregnant." "I can't get out of this car at my reunion." "I don't own a dress I could possibly wear there."

A class reunion can be hard on your union.

He might say something ridiculous like, "Why don't you be different and try to get real fat for your class reunion?"

Even if you were never noticed in high school, that night each man will act as if he's had an affair with you.

Do everything you can so it won't be the worst night of your marriage. (However, you should not ask the committee to have your husband as Master of Ceremonies if he didn't graduate that year.)

The following are a few tips on how to make your reunion better for your husband:

Limit your flirting to the time he is parking the car.

Bear in mind that people change. Your best friend in school might think that Elvis is still alive. Visit a while before you say, "Let's sit next to each other during dinner."

Laugh much harder at your husband's joke than the one your old boyfriend tells.

Make certain he doesn't find out that the piece of music you call "our song" was ever claimed by you and another.

Say, "His business card is nothing compared to your business card."

Start paying more attention to him if over five people ask, "Are you alone?"

It will be a narrow line he will have to walk. You want his jealous instincts aroused without his getting into a fight or being ornery.

Be prepared for his arguments to get out of going with you.

When he says, "I won't know anybody there," tell him the waiters and bartenders won't, either.

Have statements of persuasion ready. A few examples are:

Say, "I always had perfect attendance in high school so I don't want to spoil my record by being absent that night."

Should he say that $30.00 is too much money, tell him that if you stay until 11:30 it's only costing you 10 cents a minute.

Say, "There might be a prize for the person with the most handsome husband, and I know I would win."

Talk the reunion committee into giving a scholarship so you can tell him it's for a good cause.

It would not work to say, "I won't know how to explain your not being with me because he would provide you with an explanation such as, "Tell them I'm a con man and it wouldn't be safe to have me among them."

He might offer to send a video saying, "I'm sorry I can't be with you tonight . . ."

A night of reminiscing about times he wasn't in on could seem awfully long.

No matter how many times he asks, "You really didn't want me to come, did you?, don't stop reassuring him that you did.

Your husband could be the most charming PR man in the country and be disliked at your class reunion.

You'll know he didn't go over well with your classmates if you ask for a doggy bag and someone says, "Why didn't you bring your dog and leave your husband home?"

A couple of signals that your husband is having a rotten time would be:

> He says he is going to run home and check on the kids and you live over 200 miles away.
>
> People are asked to suggest when the next reunion should be and he shouts, "In 50 years!"

Bypass the event if it falls on the date you were married. Your class reunion is not the place to go on your wedding anniversary.

Chapter 13
Quote the Hostess, "Nevermore!"

They could not stay but just dropped by —
This rule you can observe,
You've paid them back and you are through
If they nibble on one hors d'oeuvre.

Going to friends' homes is one of the nicest parts of married life, but unfortunately, having friends back to your home is necessary. You can put off entertaining only so long.

A signal you should have a party is if you haven't received an invitation in over two years — not even the kind that says, "Bring a friend."

You might think a husband would be anxious to entertain as that is a night be can drink at a party because he doesn't have to drive home. However, usually this is not the way it is.

The following are some excuses from husbands for not inviting guests:

"I'm not sure the smoke alarm batteries are still working."

"What if an affair started at our party. We'd never forgive ourselves."

The dog is too young to be put in the basement all evening."

"The dog is too old to be put in the basement all evening.

"I want to learn to play the piano first."

"Our mattress is not firm enough to hold a lot of coats."

"We can't afford the liability insurance we should carry to have a party."

"If we wait a little longer maybe some of the people we owe will be transferred."

"Let's make a deal — we go to 10 more parties and then we have one."

Getting overstaying guests to leave can be a problem.

You can't just say, "Okay, then we won't entertain" unless you want to become an ex-party goer. You must work on persuading him.

Tell him he can work into it by asking the man next door over for a beer.

Tell him he can take the guests to the basement and show them his new saw.

Tell him how much it costs ducking into stores to avoid meeting people you owe.

Tell him the more people you have the less it will cost for heat.

Hopefully he won't say, "Oh, all right, but don't invite me!"

Making up your guest list is the most important part of planning a party. The following are a few tips:

Go through your Christmas card list and say, "We owe them. We owe them not."

Don't invite people who are just post surgery or just post trip.

Don't invite anyone running for office.

Don't ask anyone who has recently been on a cruise. They will expect too much of the food.

Let your husband know that once the invitations are sent he is committed. For example, he can't call it off if he puts his back out putting the leaves in the table.

He might even be so skittish about giving a party that after two people are there and the doorbell rings he will yell, "Don't answer that!"

It helps if you remain calm. Try to treat the day you are having a party as any other day.

Make recipes from a beginner's cookbook and hide the fact they are simple by giving them a foreign name.

Only clean parts of your house that your guests will see. If you don't turn on TV there is no danger of hearing storm warnings that will get everyone into the basement.

People have a better time if you give prizes. Think of novel reasons for giving them such as a prize to the couple paying their baby-sitter the highest rate or a prize for the couple getting the most calls from home.

It is a definite no-no to give your hostess gifts as prizes.

It will be harder to get your husband to entertain another time if guests overstay, and he feels dragged out all the next day.

Therefore, it is wise to have some ways to get company to leave. The following are a few suggestions:

Put an amplifier on your cuckoo clock.

Get up and tear the date off the calendar.

If it is cold weather, offer to go out and warm up their cars.

Let the dog up from the basement. (No matter how late it is don't say, "Sic 'em!")

Go to the freezer and get them some ice cream to take home with them.

Entertaining is expensive. Only politicians expect money from people they invite to dinner.

Chapter 14

Don't Give Your Child Brand Names and His Generic

His kids are so naughty
They break every rule
The only good that can come
They'll be kept after school.

If his children did the matchmaking between you and your husband or if you followed a girlfriend they really hated, there's a chance that you won't have problems with your stepchildren. Otherwise, look for at least a little trouble. The cases of distress-free second marriages with offspring are almost non-existent.

It is like show business with his child being a critic who gives you a bad review. It is your objective to make your husband see that the critic is wrong.

Being a stepmother is a rough tour of duty. Stepchildren will often try to sabotage the marriage. Sometimes it is subtle, like, "I can't for the life of me figure out what Elaine sees in that dry cleaning man," and sometimes obvious such as, "If Elaine's going to be at the dinner table, I won't be there!"

If you made all of your canisters into cookie jars, you still wouldn't win their affection. Even though both parents are happily re-married, they feel their Mom and Dad can get back together.

Children often make life difficult for a stepmother.

You are the star of their nightmares and 95% of the material in their diaries. They are very apt to compare the money you get from their father with their allowance.

Your husband will notice if you push your kids higher in the swing than you push his. He will think the wastebasket is always fuller when you ask his children to empty it than when you ask your children to empty it. He might say, "You didn't sterilize the needle to get the sliver out of my kid and you always do for yours."

You will never get credit from their mother for your care of them. You could have toilet trained the child, gotten him over thumb sucking, and have had the pediatrician's phone number tatooed on your hand, and she will still feel you are unfit. She is apt to send along cloth diapers for you to use, pretending she is ecology minded, and use throw-aways herself.

If his children do things that make it impossible for you to delight in them, it is important that you hide your feelings from your husband.

When he discusses his children, pretend he is talking about your children so you can make favorable comments.

Show him how red your hands are after you clapped for his child's performance.

Instead of saying to your husband, "That's a lie!" say, "The little darling must be imagining things."

When they ask you to invest in one of their schemes just decline. Don't report them to the Better Business Bureau.

There are other no-no's:

Don't say to your husband, "Let's face it — your kids are losers!"

Don't let your kids stay up longer than you let **his** kids.

Don't yawn when your husband is talking about his children.

Don't make New Year's resolutions for them.

Don't threaten to sue them for ruining your happiness.

Stepmothers usually make an all-out effort to have a good relationship with their stepchildren. One stepmother got contact lenses the color of her stepdaughter's eyes to feel closer to her.

The following are a few suggestions that could help you in your role of stepmother:

Be sure you have your morning coffee before you wake up your stepchildren.

Have a sign that reads HAVE YOU HUGGED YOUR STEPCHILD TODAY on your make-up mirror.

If you are younger than his son, have the son grow a beard the minute he can.

If their mother asks for a recipe for something they loved at your house, when you give it to her leave out, double, or halve several of the ingredients.

Only tell your husband the good things about his kids. Let him find out the bad from teachers, neighbors or the police.

Have a big celebration for his children's birthdays. You can secretly consider it a celebration for yourself, because they are getting older and will be out of the house.

Pay them for every day they get through without saying, "You're not my mother!"

If your husband doesn't believe you when you tell him what his kids do, get a camcorder.

Try to be positive in your feelings about his children. For instance, tell yourself it wasn't his children who gave you those stretch marks.

When taking pictures, be sure there are as many taken of his children as there are of your children. If there aren't, make sure you are the one who picks up the packet of developed pictures.

You shouldn't expect a bread and butter letter from your stepkids after every stay with you.

Chapter 15

To Love, Worship and Obey

Her behavior in bed is perfect
She is always the best of lovers
And if she is going to read
It's by flashlight under the covers.

When the word "obey" was still in the marriage ceremony, the most important thing a woman could do was strive to be a perfect wife.

Today, a wife is intent upon making sure she doesn't overdo.

The following are a few examples of a modern woman being certain she is getting her entitlements:

She makes one-half of the bed.

She peels the potatoes, and her husband slices them.

She folds two folds of a towel, and he does the other two.

She puts the teaspoons of instant coffee in their cups and he stirs.

If you would care to return to the ways of the former era, you could benefit from some examples of a perfect wife:

A perfect wife sees to it the gas is always on F when her husband gets in the car.

She has an amplifier by the bed so she can hear his snoring in the living room when he takes a nap or goes to bed before she does.

She cools his soup by whistling his college fight song.

She always knows the word he asks for when he's doing a crossword puzzle.

When one of their children does something wrong, she comes up with one of her ancestors who possessed the offensive trait.

When he finishes one of his oft-repeated narratives, she says, "I always hate to have that story end."

She gets HIS and HER scales and has his read less than actual weight.

She is even more agreeable during PMS.

Always blame children's undesirable traits on your relatives.

She composes and types his Thank You notes so he only has to sign them.

She takes the phone off the hook and tapes OUT OF ORDER over the doorbell when he's taking a nap.

She makes his golf trophy the centerpiece at a dinner party.

When he gets up to go to the bathroom in the middle of the night, she fluffs his pillow.

When he misspells a word, she says that is the third choice spelling.

She serves beef fillet and passes it off as meat from her husband's deer.

If her husband has a rule not to drink before 6:00 P.M., she'll have his martini ready at 5:00 and set the clock ahead.

When her husband assembles something, she tears the sentence, "Even a child can do it," off the instructions.

When she leaves the bathroom she puts up the toilet seat.

She signs her husband's name as well as hers when he doesn't accompany her to a wedding or funeral.

If he buys her a cheap sweater, she'll say, "You **darling,** you remembered I'm allergic to cashmere.

There are some things that a perfect wife does not do:

She never talks during a football game except to ask if he wants more beer.

She never gives more correct answers during a quiz show than he does.

She doesn't ask him to put the top up on a convertible when he picks her up at the beauty parlor.

She never has a charge on a statement that isn't from the current month.

She never thinks her husband is flirting but feels he is just making sure **both** sexes enjoy his great personality.

She never changes the subject when he is talking.

When he doesn't utter a word all evening she doesn't say, "What's wrong?"

A perfect wife is happier giving her husband carrots than she would be having him give her carats.

Chapter 16

Marriage Counselors Do Not Make House Calls but Police Do

When it's time for the two o'clock feeding
And you're mad 'cuz he's sleeping in bed,
Tell yourself, "This is much better
Than if he were in town painting it red."

Today's woman must have marriage counseling, because she no longer gets her frustrations out by kneading dough.

As the years pass and the excitement of love has left, the behavior of your spouse may cause you to think that you would be happier without him. What used to be cute now makes you want to give him the boot.

Maybe you no longer communicate—if you were on salt-free diets, there wouldn't be one word said during mealtime.

Perhaps he controls the TV, and you see as many as 20 different programs within half an hour.

The following are a few signals to show you that you should call for an appointment with a marriage counselor:

> There are more women's voices on the answering machine with messages for him than for you.

> He remembers Arbor day but forgets your anniversary.

One spouse wanted a cat and the other a dog so the marriage counselor suggested they get a cat and name it Rover.

He examines your marriage license to see if there is an expiration date.

He tries to prove by a blood test he isn't the father of your child who is 18.

He tapes something over your wedding video.

Marriage counselors do wonderful things. One couple was in a violent argument about getting a pet — she wanted a cat, and he wanted a dog. The counselor got them to compromise. They got a cat, named it Rover and taught it to roll over.

Counselors tell couples it's possible to order pizzas with two separate toppings, and they let them know there are electric blankets with dual controls.

There is an expression, "Don't fix what ain't broke," but the problem is deciding whether or not the marriage is "broke."

It may be that something your husband says or does might seem to you to be cause for divorce, when it really is a triviality that should be dismissed quickly from your mind. On the other hand, it could be something bad enough to need a marriage counselor's help.

The following are some examples of things of no cause for concern and those which are cause for concern:

NO BIG DEAL	BIG DEAL
He says he needs more closet space.	He says he needs more space.
He refuses to ask for directions.	He stops beautiful women to ask for directions when he really knows the way.
He doesn't say, "God bless you" when you sneeze.	You sneeze because he won't turn up the heat when you're cold.
He leaves the cap off the toothpaste.	He never takes the cap off the toothpaste.
He doesn't use the right fork.	He never uses a fork.
He doesn't carry a picture of you in his billfold.	He takes embarrassing candid shots of you and shows them to everyone.
He says you need a therapist.	He says you need an exorcist.

NO BIG DEAL	BIG DEAL
He brought a friend of his home for dinner without calling you first.	He brought your former boyfriend home for dinner without calling you first.
He hogs the covers.	The covers he is hogging are from another woman.
He didn't bring a souvenir for you from his trip.	He never returned from his trip.
He never listens to what you say.	He repeats what you say at his poker club for laughs.

When you decide a marriage counselor is a must, you won't find it easy to get your husband to go to one with you. The following are a few suggestions of how to accomplish this difficult feat:

Lie and tell him his sports hero has had marriage counseling.

Ask him, "Don't you ever want people to clap when you say how long you've been married?"

Tell him, "You can go and just stand outside and listen through the door."

Give him a gift certificate to a marriage counselor.

Realize you have trouble if he refuses to go to a marriage counselor with a hyphenated name.

If it is impossible to get him there tell yourself, "Martyrs go straight to heaven."

Chapter 17

Tell Yourself He's Just on Vacation

More than one C.E.O.
Has turned into a cabbie
When after retirement
His wife found him crabby.

The time your husband is gone away from home all day is fleeting. You can't believe how fast his retirement arrives.

Marriage is full of adjustment but never so much as when your husband retires.

You shouldn't feel there is something wrong with your marriage because you hate your spouse's retirement. This is natural and has nothing to do with your love for your mate.

However, you can and should work at making this time more pleasant for both of you.

Naturally, you will put off his being home all day as long as possible.

The following are a few statements that could possibly make him consider postponing the day he says good-bye to his co-workers:

"You may be shown up by your replacement."

"You have too many neckties."

"Wouldn't it be nice to earn the record of staying with your company the longest."

"Isn't it nicer to have other people than just me sniff your great smelling after-shave lotion."

"You'll miss getting those Christmas presents from the people you supervise."

"The radio program you enjoyed during your drive home won't be as much fun to listen to when you're not in the car."

It would be all right if your husband would be bored and just yawned, but boredom of a retired man often leads to irritability.

Fertilize the lawn so he has to mow more frequently.

Therefore, you must think about keeping him busy. The following are a few suggestions:

Buy things unassembled and unpainted.

Drive the car places where it will get dirty, and he will have to wash it.

Get him a Ten Most Wanted list and have him sit in the mall to try and spot one of them. Tell him he can do whatever he wants with the reward.

Fertilize the lawn so he has to mow more frequently.

Buy a car with a small gas tank so he has to get gas more often. Men tend to hang around a service station after they fill up.

Talk him into taking an art course. Tell him you'll give him equal space with the grandchildren on the refrigerator.

Put your savings into a lot of different stocks, and tell him it is important that he attend every stockholders' meeting.

Give your dog a lot of water.

Suggest he write a romance novel. This could even perk up your sex life.

Point out NOW HIRING signs, and pretend you're interested for a grandchild.

Tell him to visit your children. Say, "Since you were at work when your own kids had "firsts," it would be nice if you caught some of the "firsts" of your grandchildren.

Minutes add up to hours so never dismiss any idea you have to keep him occupied no matter how little of his time it will take.

Buy him sweaters with a lot of buttons.

Have him put the mail in alphabetical order before he hands it to you.

If your electric door opener breaks, don't get it fixed.

Have him scrub his dentures instead of soaking them overnight.

There are things you should not do in handling retirement:

Don't make his first chore list after you get home from his retirement party. Wait until the next morning.

Don't be sarcastic and say, "It's too bad we didn't take before and after pictures to see how much better the house looks after you're home to show me how to do things."

Don't let him phone to find out if a store has an item. Let his feet, not his fingers, do the walking.

Don't worry when he's out of the house for a long time that he's hanging out with the wrong people. He is not going to join a gang.

If he has a part-time job don't suggest he get one more part-time job.

It is most important that you never let your husband feel you are anything but happy about his working days being at an end.

For instance, it would be terrible if you called your friends, whose husbands are retired, your support group.

After all, there **are** many advantages to this phase of life:

When you fight in the morning, you don't have to wait eight hours to make up.

You don't have to worry about him having an affair with his secretary when he doesn't have a secretary.

On days when you're expecting a repairman, you can leave the house, because your husband will be there.

You don't have to worry about giving him the same thing for dinner that he had for lunch because you made his lunch.

It would be a nice idea to celebrate the anniversary of his retirement.

Merry Marriage Memories